HALLUCINOGENS

Hallucinogens twist the way users see the world around them.

HALLUCINOGENS

Ann Ricki Hurwitz
Sue Hurwitz

THE ROSEN PUBLISHING GROUP, INC.
NEW YORK

The people pictured in this book are only models; they in no way practice or endorse the activities illustrated. Captions serve only to explain the subjects of photographs and do not in any way imply a connection between the real-life models and the staged situations.

Published in 1992, 1996 by The Rosen Publishing Group, Inc.
29 East 21st Street, New York, NY 10010

Revised Edition, 1996

Printed in the United States of America.

Library of Congress Cataloging-in-Publication Data

Hurwitz, Ann Ricki
    Hallucinogens / by Ann Ricki Hurwitz and
    Sue Hurwitz.—rev. ed.
    (The Drug Abuse Prevention Library)
    Includes bibliographical references and index.
    Summary: Describes psilocybin, LSD, mescaline, and
    other hallucinogenic drugs and discusses their
    dangerous and destructive effects.
        ISBN 0-8239-2103-4
        1. Hallucinogenic drugs—Juvenile literature. 2.
    [1. Hallucinogenic drugs. 2. Drugs. 3. Drug
    abuse.] I. Hurwitz, Ann Ricki. II. Title.
    III. Series
    HV5809.5.H87 1996
    362.29'4—dc20
                         92-8599
                           CIP
                           AC

Contents

Introduction

*I*n the past year, studies have shown
that the number of young people in the
United States who are using hallucinogens
is increasing. These drugs, including
marijuana (pot) and LSD (acid), change
the way users feel, see, hear, smell, and
think. Hallucinogens cause users to
hallucinate, to hear and see things that
are not there. They are illegal.

There are serious dangers in using
these drugs because they change a user's
perception of reality. When a user does
not perceive things normally, he or she
does not react normally. Teens often
choose not to use them because of the
risks involved. Many young people say
they do not use hallucinogens because
they don't want to upset the chemicals in
their brains. Others do not like the way
hallucinogens make them feel. In

addition, these drugs are very expensive. Maintaining an addiction is costly.

Taking hallucinogens also means risking unpleasant side effects: the terror of bad trips; addiction; and permanent damage to the body and mind. This book examines a wide range of hallucinogenic drugs. It discusses how they can affect your mind and how they can affect the lives of the people who use them.

A teenager's life is filled with pressure. You may have heard that using drugs will help ease that pressure. That is not true. Using any hallucinogen, even if it is "just smoking pot," actually makes things more difficult to handle, especially if you become addicted. There are better ways to solve problems. Growing up in the '90s puts enough of a strain on your brain *without* taking drugs to increase your confusion and anxiety.

In fact, confusion and anxiety are usually what hallucinogens create in the minds of user. This not only affects the user, but those around him or her. Losing control of your life places tremendous strain on your friends and family, or anyone who cares about you. And it prevents you from caring about yourself.

Many hallucinogens are made from plants like the peyote cactus.

CHAPTER 1

Hallucinogens— What They Are and What They Do

*T*here are many kinds of drugs. Some are legal and are used to help cure illnesses. Some are illegal and can only harm people. Some drugs are natural; that is, they occur in the world. They are plants, or parts of plants. Other drugs are human-made. They are made in laboratories by scientists. Some human-made drugs are legal and useful. Others are illegal and very dangerous. Hallucinogens fall into the illegal-and-dangerous category.

10 | *Natural Hallucinogens*

Magic Mushrooms

Mushrooms are plants called *fungi*. Fungi live on living or dead plants. Mushrooms grow all around the world. There are thousands of kinds of mushrooms. The kind that you find in grocery stores are safe and are also good for you.

But some mushrooms are poisonous and can kill you. Some mushrooms—called magic mushrooms—contain a chemical called *psilocybin*. This natural chemical is a hallucinogen.

Magic mushrooms may be eaten fresh, cooked, dried, or crushed. Usually they are swallowed in tablets or capsules.

The psilocybin in magic mushrooms causes users to see, hear, and feel things in ways that are not normal. Often users see very colorful hallucinations. They may feel light-headed or so relaxed that nothing seems to matter. Psilocybin may also cause diarrhea and stomach cramps.

The effects of magic mushrooms begin in about 15 minutes and may last 9 hours. Sometimes users have flashbacks.

Mescaline

Peyote is a short, spineless cactus plant. It grows in the deserts of Mexico and the

southwestern United States. The top of
the cactus has a little crown or button.
This button contains a chemical called
mescaline.

11

Slices of the peyote crown may be eaten
fresh or dried into hard, brown buttons.
The buttons are often swallowed whole or
used to make tea. Peyote buttons can be
kept for many years.

Mescaline can also be made by humans.
Human-made mescaline is most often
found in capsules or tablets.

Mescaline changes the way the brain
works. It causes users to see things, especially
colors, that are not real. Mescaline can
cause hallucinations.

About an hour after using mescaline,
trippers may have physical effects such as
nausea and vomiting. They may have
ragged breathing, increased heart rate, or
the shakes. Sometimes the pupils of the
eyes are dilated, or enlarged. The effects
of mescaline have been known to last up
to 12 hours.

Mescaline, or peyote, has been known
as a mind-changing drug for hundreds of
years. The Aztecs of South America used
peyote in religious ceremonies. Even
today some Native Americans want to use
it in their religious ceremonies.

12 | Marijuana

Marijuana is sometimes called "pot" or "grass." Marijuana is a drug made from the cannabis, or hemp, plant. This plant grows in warm climates all over the world, including the United States.

The cannabis plant contains more than 400 chemicals. Many of the chemicals stay in a user's body for months. *Tetrahydrocannabinol*, or THC, is the chemical in marijuana that is a hallucinogen.

Marijuana may be added to food or brewed into tea. Usually it is smoked in handmade cigarettes called "joints," "sticks," or "reefers." Smoking one joint of marijuana is as harmful as smoking five cigarettes made of tobacco.

Marijuana may injure both the body and the mind. When smoking marijuana, the tripper holds in the smoke as long as possible. That is very harmful to the lungs. Long-term use may cause lung cancer and heart disease. Marijuana is harmful to the white blood cells, which help fight off disease. Many users become sick more often than nonusers.

Marijuana changes the way the brain works. The effects of marijuana begin about 15 to 30 minutes after using it.

Many people suffer serious side effects from taking drugs.

14 Trippers may feel relaxed, drowsy, or happy. They may have mild hallucinations for several hours. When that happens the user is said to be "high," or "stoned."

Some users find it hard to think clearly or to remember things. They may become moody, easily upset, and unable to pay attention. They may talk and giggle more than usual. That makes it hard to learn at school or on the job. Sometimes they have panic reactions and feel that their lives are out of control.

Drugs do not affect everyone the same way. Doctors still do not know all the long-term effects of using marijuana. But doctors do know that long-time users of marijuana often become dependent on it. They need more and more marijuana just to feel normal.

Long-term use of marijuana damages the brain and nervous system. Users may never think in a normal way again.

Human-Made Hallucinogens
LSD
LSD, or *lysergic acid diethylamide,* is sometimes called "acid." LSD is found on a fungus that grows on rye and other grains. It is also one of the most powerful

drugs made by humans. LSD is 100 times
stronger than magic mushrooms. It is
more than 4,000 times stronger than
mescaline.

LSD is a tasteless, colorless, odorless
white powder. It is made into tablets, or
capsules, or a liquid. Liquid LSD can be
swallowed by putting it onto sugar cubes,
gelatin, blotting paper, stamps, or candy.
Acid may also be injected into a vein.

LSD changes the way the brain works.
Usually a user feels the effects 30 to 90
minutes after taking it. The effects can
last up to 12 hours. Taking a dose of LSD
is called "tripping."

The mental effects of LSD are similar to
those of the other hallucinogens, but even
stronger. A tripper may begin to feel several
different emotions at once. There is no
way to tell at the start if it will be a "good
trip" or a "bad trip."

On a bad trip a user's mind may swing
rapidly from one wild emotion to another.
These changes can be frightening and
make users feel helpless. Sometimes users
think they can attempt superhuman or
dangerous things. Sometimes they feel
panic, confusion, anxiety, or that their
lives are out of control.

16   The physical effects of LSD are sweating, loss of appetite, sleeplessness, dry mouth, and the shakes. LSD may also raise the body temperature, heart rate, and blood pressure. The pupils of the eyes may become dilated.

LSD is so powerful that its effects may never leave the mind or body. Doctors think that LSD may injure children born to users. Trippers often have flashbacks years later even if they never use LSD again.

PCP

PCP, or *phencyclidine,* is sometimes called "angel dust" or "killer weed." PCP is the most dangerous hallucinogen. It is also the one most widely used. Trippers often become physically dependent on PCP. Long-term use may cause brain damage.

PCP was developed as a medicine to put people to sleep or to block pain during surgical operations. But doctors soon learned that it causes confusion, halluci-nations, anxiety, and even seizures. PCP is *not* a legal drug today.

PCP is made into a pure, white crystal-like powder. It may be swallowed in tablets or capsules, sniffed, or injected.

The only sure way to avoid getting hooked on drugs is to refuse them.

Hallucinogens can cause violent and unpredictable changes in mood.

Ecstasy is made in illegal labs, so users never can be sure what is in the pills or capsules they buy. The effects of ecstasy are similar to those of LSD. Many times users really get LSD when they pay for ecstasy.

Besides hallucinations, ecstasy may cause depression, nervousness, nausea, and vomiting. The effects of ecstasy begin about 30 minutes after use and may last 4 hours. Like most hallucinogens, ecstasy often causes negative reactions rather than positive ones. Users may never know in advance how their bodies will react to the drugs they take.

Because drugs can change coordination and muscle control,
users are more likely to cause serious accidents or injuries.

CHAPTER 2

Some of the Dangers

*C*hanice was excited to be in New York City for the first time. She had saved up money for the trip for months. She was visiting some friends who promised to show her a great time, including a night out at one of the best nightclubs in the country. Chanice loved to dance to good music, and she was looking forward to the excitement and glamour of a club. Being only 17, she had never even gotten into a bar before. Her friends assured her that they would be able to get her into the club without her needing to show ID.

After a day of shopping and sight-seeing, Chanice had dinner and got ready to go out. She and her friends Marvely

24 and Joanne first went to a couple of parties. They arrived at the club at 2:30 a.m. Chanice was already pretty tired, so Joanne suggested a "pick-me-up" before they hit the dance floor.

"Like what?" asked Chanice.

"Well, as long as you're here, you might as well have the full night-out treatment," said Joanne. "Would you like to try ecstasy?"

Chanice was uncertain, but curious. "What does it do?" she asked.

"You'll feel really happy and energetic, and you'll want to dance and hug people a lot," said Marvely. "Don't feel pressured. You don't have to do it, but we definitely are."

Chanice didn't want to be left out of the fun, and besides, she was feeling way too tired to dance. She felt she could use some energy. "Okay, why not? How much is it?" she asked.

"It's $25 a hit," said Joanne.

Ugh, thought Chanice, there goes $25 of my vacation money. Oh well, I really do want to dance.

She watched as Joanne approached a man in a baseball cap and baggy jeans who took her money and handed her three white capsules.

"I can't believe I'm doing this," Chanice
said as she swallowed the capsule.

"Let's go sit down," suggested Marvely.

They found a place to sit in the lounge
area. Chanice talked to a few people, and
everybody seemed incredibly friendly. After
about half an hour she began to feel light-
headed.

"Whew, I think my ex is kicking in," said
Marvely.

"I'm not sure, but I think mine is too,"
said Chanice. Did I say that? she thought.
It sounded so strange. Then she giggled.
Joanne and Marvely started giggling, too.

"Yeah, this is it!" Joanne said, excited.

Suddenly Chanice felt light as a feather,
as if she were floating through the air. She
also felt very happy, and everything around
her looked beautiful. "This is a gorgeous
club! The lights are so pretty," Chanice
said.

"It is beautiful," said Marvely through
clenched teeth, her voice shaky.

They all smiled at each other for a
moment, then Joanne suggested dancing.

"Yes, let's dance!" Chanice shouted.

Chanice seemed to be drifting to the
dance floor on a wave of pleasure, and she
felt the music fill her. She danced as she'd
never danced before, feeling the beat in

26 every part of her body. They danced for four hours. Then suddenly Chanice started getting tired. She was no longer feeling exhilarated, and she was very thirsty.

"We're comin' down," said Marvely.

"I need a drink and a seat," said Chanice.

Chanice was dizzy. After fumbling with her wallet at the bar, she got a drink and stumbled to the lounge. She was so dizzy she could barely walk. The three friends thumped down at a table. Suddenly Chanice felt her entire body fall. She wasn't floating anymore. I don't want this to end, she thought. I need more. I want to be happy and high again.

"Let's do more. Can we do more?" she begged her friends.

Marvely and Joanne looked at each other and laughed. "Do you realize it's 7:00 in the morning?" said Joanne.

"It can't be!" Chanice said. She was starting to ache all over, and her thoughts were getting jumbled. "I'm going to get more."

Joanne looked annoyed. "Okay, do what you want. But we can't stay. I have to go to bed," she said.

Drugs make it hard for you to focus on anything that needs concentration.

28　　Chanice found the man in the baseball cap and gave him $100 for four capsules, then left the club with her friends. By now her ecstasy had completely worn off. She felt depressed and confused.

I just blew $100 on drugs, Chanice realized. But I want to feel that good again.

When Chanice returned home from New York, she found dealers who sold ecstasy around her school. Chanice started taking ecstasy every Saturday night and felt really high. But the more she did it, the more depressed she got in between. She became trapped in a miserable cycle of highs and lows. Chanice became dependent on ecstasy to bring her out of the depression, but each time she used ecstasy it left her even more depressed later, which made her crave ecstasy even more.

She couldn't focus on school. She alienated her friends, who couldn't understand why she was always sad and irritable. She spent more and more time alone. Finally, her father confronted her. He asked if she was using drugs. She denied it. But a week later, while buying ecstasy from a dealer, she was arrested. Chanice had let drugs rule her life.

Carlo Said Yes to Mescaline

Carlo loved horses. Three years ago, when he was 12, he began working on his uncle's ranch. He fed the horses early, gave them water, and brushed them down.

Carlo often went riding after he finished work. Midnight was his favorite horse. Carlo would ride Midnight to the far end of the ranch. He loved feeling the wind against his face. He loved the fresh smell of the air. And he loved being outdoors!

Sometimes Carlo took along a sleeping bag and spent the night out under the stars. He enjoyed that most of all.

Carlo's uncle hired a new ranch hand named Ken. Ken was 17. Carlo and Ken soon became friends. Sometimes they rode together after work.

"Want to try some peyote before we ride out?" Ken asked one day. "Peyote will give you beautiful visions...you will see things in new ways."

Carlo thought about the land, the grass, the flowers, the trees, the hills, and the stream where Midnight stopped to drink. Could that really look any more beautiful than it already did?

"I don't know," Carlo hedged. "I don't do drugs."

Appreciating the world's natural beauty is one way to feel great.

"Why not?" Ken asked. "The effects of mescaline last a long time. You don't need to use it more than once when you want to trip. Live a little, Carlo! Don't be so uptight!"

Carlo said no. But later he wondered what he might be missing. When he and Ken unrolled their sleeping bags, Ken tempted him again.

"I'm starting to see visions," Ken said. "Do you want a peyote button or not?"

Carlo knew he should refuse again. But perhaps once would not hurt. It had been nearly an hour since Ken took the peyote, and nothing had happened to him.

"Yes," Carlo agreed. "Give me a button." Carlo took a swig of water from his canteen to wash down the drug. Then he stretched out on his sleeping bag and waited. And waited.

Carlo stared up at the stars as he usually did. But soon the stars looked different. They glittered more brightly. They seemed bigger and closer. In fact, the stars seemed to be dropping down from the sky onto Carlo's face!

Carlo shut his eyes for a minute. When he opened them, he "saw" giant clouds swallow up the stars. The clouds were dark and scary. They were hanging down

A true friend will try to help another who is on drugs.

lower and lower. Soon they would smother him!

Carlo sat up. He ran to a nearby tree and climbed onto a branch. He began throwing leaves into the air.

"What are you doing?" Ken asked.

"I am shooting scuds at those clouds!" Carlo yelled. "Those clouds have poisonous gas. Can't you smell their terrible odor? Those clouds are trying to kill me!"

"You are having hallucinations," Ken said. "The best way to deal with a bad trip is to try to relax and calm down. Come down and try to sleep your bummer off!"

"No!" Carlo threw a handful of leaves at Ken. "You're after me too! Stay away!"

"Suit yourself," Ken said. He rolled over and studied the bright greens in a blade of grass. He had his own visions to deal with!

Carlo panicked. Could he escape from those deadly clouds? Would the clouds poison him? He wished he could think more clearly. But he felt like puking. And he was trembling so badly that he knew he could not hang onto the tree much longer.

Finally Carlo "saw" a wide river flowing under the tree. Now he could escape! He would jump into the river and swim away.

Carlo jumped.

34　　He woke up in the hospital with two broken legs and a huge bump on his head. He ached all over. But he was lucky. He was alive! And he probably would be able to walk. But the doctors were not sure if he would ever be able to ride again.

"I hope you have learned not to mess with drugs." Carlo's uncle said.

"I've learned the hard way," Carlo quietly answered. "I don't need drugs to help me see beautiful things. The world is beautiful just as it is. I'll never say yes to drugs again!"

Nikki Said Yes to Marijuana

Nikki and Robin lived next door to each other and were good friends. They went nearly everywhere together. Nikki was quiet and shy around people she did not know well. Robin was more outgoing and made new friends easily.

Both girls turned 17 and got their driver's licenses. The following weekend they went to a school basketball game. Nikki drove.

During the game Robin began talking to several older girls who sat by them. Mona, one of their new friends, invited Nikki and Robin to a party at her house after the game.

Nikki and Robin accepted. After all, what possibly could happen? Nikki had her parents' car for the evening. If the party was dull they would not even need to call home for a ride. They could just leave.

"Mona said the refreshments are big submarine sandwiches and beer," Robin told Nikki later as they drove to the party. "But I'm sure they'll have soft drinks, too."

"Don't be so sure," Nikki replied. "We don't know Mona that well. It's hard to guess what she and her friends may do."

"So we'll see," Robin answered. "If the party is in the fast lane, we'll just leave."

"Agreed!" Nikki replied.

When Nikki and Robin got to the party they were impressed. There were more boys than girls—for a change! And everyone seemed friendly.

"I'm Garth," said a cute guy standing by the refreshments. "Can I get you something to drink?"

"Do you have soda?" Robin asked. "Yes, what do you want in it?" Garth smiled.

"A few ice cubes would be great," Nikki replied. She picked up a paper plate and reached for a sandwich.

"We can do better than that!" Garth boasted. "How about a little vodka?"

36

"No, thanks," Robin replied.

"I'll pass,too," Nikki told Garth. She took the soda and balanced it on the edge of her plate while Robin got a sandwich. Then both girls looked around for a place to sit.

"Most of these guys are seniors," Robin said between sips of her soda. "I've seen them at school."

"Yeah," Nikki agreed. "And every one of them is cute!"

"Having a good time?" Mona asked as she weaved her way through the crowd.

"The sandwiches are delicious," Robin answered.

"This is Garth and Dino," Mona said. She casually introduced them to each other. "Have fun."

Garth sat down beside Nikki. Dino sat down on the other side of Robin. Garth talked about school and discussed his plans for college. Nikki was glad to listen. Then he asked her to dance.

Nikki was having a great time. Garth was a good dancer. After the first few minutes she did not even feel awkward. But she did get tired and needed to catch her breath. So they sat out the next few dances.

Teens often start smoking because of peer pressure.

38

Garth lit up a joint and offered Nikki a drag. "Want some grass?"

"No, thanks," Nikki said. "I tried pot once when I was about 12. It didn't do anything for me."

"Your grass probably didn't have much THC in it," Garth explained. He looked at the joint in his hand. "This stuff is super! Today's marijuana has more THC. It can really make you feel good!"

Garth put the joint up to Nikki's lips. "Go ahead," he urged. "Take a drag."

Nikki knew she should say no again. But she liked Garth. She hoped he would ask her for a date. She didn't want him to think she was a baby. Besides, she had tried pot before and nothing bad had happened.

So Nikki said yes and inhaled deeply. She held in the smoke as long as she could. Then she let it escape slowly from her lips. She felt like coughing, but instead she cleared her throat.

After Garth finished the joint, he and Nikki began dancing again.

Now Nikki felt as if she were walking through a dream. Everything Garth said seemed so funny that she could not stop giggling. She kept stepping on Garth's toes and giggling even more.

"My feet seem to have a mind of their own," Nikki said. "Are you sure you didn't spike my soda with alcohol?"

"It's the pot," Garth insisted. "It's making you feel slightly drunk."

"Umm," Nikki said. "I didn't think anyone could get *slightly* drunk."

When the record ended, Robin came over to Nikki. "We should leave now," she insisted. "It's getting late."

"Okay," Nikki said. "Goodbye, Garth."

"I'll call you, Nikki," Garth promised.

As they walked to the car Robin said, "Give me your car keys. I'll drive."

"Forget it," Nikki snapped back. "I'm perfectly capable of driving!"

"Look, Nikki," Robin said. "I saw you smoke pot. I know you're high. Your reflexes are so affected that you could hardly dance! Let me drive."

"We are only 10 blocks from home," Nikki pouted. "Nothing will happen."

Nikki got behind the wheel and started the car. As she pulled away from the curb she almost sideswiped several parked cars.

"Some people don't know how to park!" she complained to Robin. She did not say that the cars looked blurry and their shapes seemed to keep changing.

Drugs change the way you experience reality and make it very dangerous to do things that require good judgment.

"Please let me drive, Nikki," Robin
pleaded. "I'll be careful with your parents'
car."

"I can do it," Nikki insisted. "We'll be
there in a few minutes!"

Nikki tried to stop when they came to a
traffic light. But her foot could not find
the brake pedal. Nikki drove through the
red light.

They were hit by a car that started to
cross the intersection on the green light.

Brakes squealed. Cars twisted around
each other. Glass broke and flew. Blood
splattered. Bones were crushed. Cries of
pain were heard everywhere.

Robin ended up in the hospital with
seven broken ribs and several cuts and
bruises.

But Nikki was not so lucky. She was
dead on arrival at the hospital.

"Nikki should never have said yes to
marijuana," Robin moaned between sobs
to her parents. "Nikki was my friend...
she was a good person. She just made a
foolish mistake."

John Said Yes to LSD

John's introduction to heavy drugs came at
a very young age. He did LSD for the first

42 time when he was 16. He didn't know a lot about drugs; he thought it was cool to do drugs. He was in a band, and the band members would all trip together. They all thought it improved their music.

John was really enjoying the hallu-cinations and the energy, just having fun with it. He had no idea you could have a *bad* trip. That is, until it actually hap-pened.

It was a Saturday night at around 12:30 a.m. The band members were hanging out in the practice room. They had each taken a hit of acid about an hour ago, and it still had not kicked in. George, the lead singer, suggested that they take more. John was bored, so he agreed. But as soon as they swallowed the second hit, the first one took effect—and it came on strong.

It was the strongest stuff John had ever done. He was nervous. *One* hit was almost too much to take. How was he going to deal with two?

The more he thought about it, the more panicked he became. He suddenly started sweating and felt sick to his stomach. He thought everyone was out to get him and was afraid talk to any of his band-mates. He just didn't trust them; they

seemed scary. They saw that John was
freaking out and tried to help, but the
more they talked to him, the more frightening they seemed.

Bill, the drummer, suggested that if John
ate something it might help him come
down. He gave John a slice of white bread
and a glass of orange soda. John managed
to unclench his jaw and shoved a piece of
the bread between his shaking lips. He
didn't realize how dry his mouth had
become—there was almost no saliva in it.
The bread stuck in his throat. He tried to
wash it down with the soda, which tasted
like sugar and bitter chemicals.

Soon he felt the nervous rush of the
second hit washing over him, sweeping
him even further away from reality. John
feared that he had gone completely insane
and would never come back. He couldn't
see anything. Everything was just a blur
of color.

John was disoriented. He had lost all
concept of time. At one point it seemed to
him that things were happening over and
over again. The same song seemed to be
playing on the radio for hours, when it
actually only played once. Everything kept
"looping" that way, again and again. All he
wanted was for this nightmare to end, but

44 he was tripping so hard it seemed to last forever.

John knew a lot of people who always took acid at Grateful Dead concerts. They had talked about the love and harmony everybody shared while high on the drug. So why was he so afraid? He was terrified of his friends. He thought they were plotting against him, and he knew he had to get away from them before they hurt him. When he finally managed to get to his feet, he stumbled to the bathroom and locked the door. He sat in the bathtub in total darkness for the rest of the night, waiting for the terror to subside.

John woke up the next morning incredibly sore and unable to think clearly. He snuck out of the house, too embarrassed to say good-bye to his sleeping bandmates. When he got home, he realized he must look awful, because his mother gave him a funny look.

"Rough night?" she asked, putting groceries away.

John's brain searched for a response, but he couldn't think of anything. Rough night? What did she know? Was she playing some weird mind game? He couldn't answer. His mother put down her groceries and stared at him, concerned.

The rise in drug use in America has also caused a sharp rise in the country's crime rate. Most of this crime is committed by users who need to support their habit.

46 Why couldn't he answer her? "Stop looking at me!" he thought.

"We stayed up late practicing," John finally blurted out. Fortunately, she didn't push it, and John escaped to his bedroom and slept for the rest of the day.

John wished someone had warned him that LSD use could cause him to have terrifying experiences like the one he had. He promised himself that he would not say yes to drugs again.

Molly Said Yes to PCP

Both of Molly's parents had to work long hours. Molly was often at home alone. When she was younger, she played outside with other kids in the neighborhood. But now she spent more time alone. She was usually inside watching TV or doing homework.

Molly's older brother, Marco, was 17. Marco often stayed out late or he did not come home at all. On weekends he and his friends usually drank beer and did drugs on the back porch.

Marco usually stayed away from Molly, but when she turned 12, Marco gave her a drag off his PCP joint as a birthday present.

Molly became very excited and started acting crazy. She climbed onto the swing that hung from a tree and started doing dangerous stunts. Molly fell off the swing many times and scraped her arms and knees. But she did not feel any pain, so she let her wounds bleed and kept showing off.

After that, Molly joined her brother and his friends when they smoked joints laced with PCP. Soon she became hooked.

Molly began having trouble at school. She could not think straight or remember things. She often got mad at her teachers and was very rude. Her classmates also got on her nerves. Molly would push them out of the way when she walked down the halls. Everyone began to avoid Molly.

The school principal sent a letter to Molly's parents requesting a conference, and her mother was furious.

"Are you in some kind of trouble?" she asked, showing Molly the letter.

"No," Molly replied. "It's just that the teachers don't like me. They're on my case for nothing!"

Molly's mother asked a school counselor to have a phone conference since she could not get time off from work.

"The counselor told Mother that you are moody and rude and failing most of your

Sudden failing grades are sometimes a sign of drug use.

classes," Molly's father reported. "You're grounded until you straighten this out!"

Grounded? Molly almost laughed. She did not have any friends to run around with anymore. They had all dropped her. And she did not care. When she was not smoking PCP with Marco and his buddies, she slept. So what if she was grounded?

Molly knew she should lay off the drugs for a while and pay more attention to her schoolwork. But it was too late. She could not get through the week without her PCP at least every other day.

Molly was not quite 13, and she was sick of always being on the wrong side of the rules. First at school, and now at home. Maybe she needed help. Maybe she should tell her mom. But her dad would kill her if he knew she did drugs!

One weekend Marco and his friends and Molly were high on PCP. The boys began arguing about getting money for more drugs. They punched each other around. One of them pulled a knife and cut Marco on the arm. They complained that Molly did not do her share to bring in money. Then they told her that they were going to rob a gas station at midnight and she had to come along.

50

"I didn't know you broke the law to buy drugs," Molly told Marco. "Why didn't you tell me before?"

"Don't worry, Molly. I'll take care of it," Marco insisted. "I don't want you to get involved in this."

"But I am involved!" Molly pouted. "I want to help!"

Molly was sent into the gas station to buy a bag of chips. She was pretty nervous, and she felt a little dizzy. But she was fearless. She felt as if she could handle the robbery all by herself if necessary.

When Molly went to the check out, the manager rang up her purchase. While the cash register was open, Marco and two of his friends burst through the door and demanded money.

The station manager set off an alarm, and the noise sent Marco into a rage. Marco started spraying the room with bullets. He yelled something, but his words were slurred. Molly could not tell if he was talking to her or trying to scare the manager. Marco shot the manager just as the manager drew a pistol and shot Marco.

"Come on," the boys shouted at Molly as they ran out the door. "Leave him!"

Small crimes, like stealing from home, often lead drug users to larger crimes that support their growing habit.

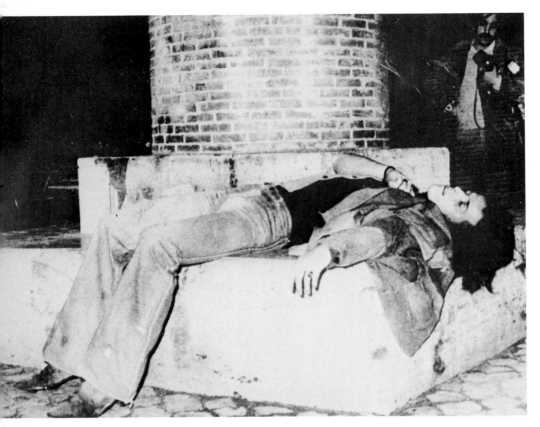

Many drug users lose control of their lives.

But Molly was horrified. She could not leave her brother dying on the floor. She bent down and held Marco's head in her lap. She kept calling his name. When the police arrived they had to pull a screaming Molly away from her dead brother.

Molly's father later told her that she had been fingerprinted and had spent the night 52 | in jail. But Molly did not remember any of it. The last thing she remembered was the look in Marco's eyes when he went into that rage.

Molly even blocked out most of the time she spent in the hospital and later in the halfway house. Because of her age, Molly was not sent to prison, but she now had a criminal record.

By the time Molly straightened out her problems with the law she was 14. And she felt rotten. Because she was still on probation, she had to live at home. And she had to go to school. Molly was so depressed that she wanted to stop living.

Marco was dead. His friends were in prison. Molly felt guilty, too. She had no friends of her own. Her parents blamed her for Marco's death, and they did not talk to her. Big deal! They were never home anyway! Now the only person Molly ever saw was her parole officer.

Molly hated her life. She slept through most of her classes. When she did stay awake, she got into trouble with other students or with her teachers. She spent more time waiting outside the principal's office than she did in the classroom.

Molly simply couldn't cope with her life without drugs.

54

But she needed money to buy drugs. So Molly began selling her body to get money for drugs. She knew that sleeping around was as dangerous as doing drugs. But by now she did not care. She had absolutely no self-respect. Her self-image could not have been lower if she had pulled the gun and shot Marco herself.

Molly looked up some of Marco's old friends. They sold her drugs. When they could not get PCP, she bought whatever they had. They often sold her ecstasy, which they claimed was even better than PCP. She did not care what she used as long as it kept her from thinking about her problems and her life.

Molly soon overdosed. Was it on purpose? Or did the drugs she bought poison her?

Molly was 14 when she died. She had used PCP for two years and other drugs for about three months. She did not want to say yes again to drugs. But she did not have the courage to say no.

Molly was so confused that she did not even try to get help. She could have gone to a clinic or a hospital for therapy to help kick her drug habit. She could have asked for help at school. She could have asked her parents to help her. Her friends might have kept her from feeling so lonely, if she had had any friends.

But Molly could not think clearly. She could not see an end to the mess her life had become. Molly became one of a huge number of people who die from using drugs every year.

Molly let drugs destroy her life.

Parents, teachers, friends, and counselors are just a few of the
people who can help teens work out their problems.

CHAPTER 3

Knowledge is Power

*A*lthough we can predict the effects of certain drugs in most people, drugs create different reactions in different people. This makes hallucinogens all the more dangerous. For example, LSD usually makes a user see bright colors and psychedelic images, but it can make some users see grotesque, terrifying scenes of violence. There is no way of knowing for sure how any hallucinogenic drug will affect you. Sometimes even one dose can kill. It is also possible that you may not have a bad trip the first one or two times you try a drug. However, heavy use of hallucinogens can result in brain damage or mental illness.

58

Another risk is not knowing what is truly in the drugs that are sold on the streets. Because these drugs are illegal, there are no laws regulating their purity. Dealers eager to make more money may cut ecstasy with other substances. This dilution happens frequently with other drugs as well.

There is no "safe" way to take hallucinogens. The risks of using hallucinogens are many, and there are no lasting rewards. All drugs are poisonous if used in large enough dosage.

Use of hallucinogens can damage your mind and body. You can become a slave to a drug. You can become a slave to drug dealers. You can be haunted by flashbacks. You can be arrested if caught in possession of hallucinogens.

Do you really need these problems in your life? Could hallucinogens possibly be worth what they might cost you? Consider these questions carefully.

If you are a user, and you want to quit, people are available to help you. Page 59 lists places you can contact for assistance and information.

You can become drug-free. Learn the facts, then decide what is best for you.

Help List

Associations

American Council for
  Drug Education
1225 North King Street
Wilmington, DE 19801
(302) 658-7237

National Council on
  Alcoholism and Drug
  Dependency
40 West 38th Street
New York, NY 10018
24-Hour Hotline:
1-800-622-2255

National Institute on Drug
  Abuse (NIDA)
NIDA Information and
  Treatment Center
5600 Fischer Lane
Rockville, MD 20852
Hotline: 1-800-662-HELP

Narcotics Anonymous
World Service Office
16155 Wyandotte Street
Van Nuys, CA 91406

Canada

Council on Drug Abuse
698 Weston Road
Toronto, ON M6N 3R3

Alcohol and Drug Depen-
  dency Information and
  Counseling Services
  (ADDICS)
#2, 24711/2 Portage
  Avenue
Winnipeg, MB R3J 0N6
204-831-1999

Narcotics Anonymous
P.O. Box 7500
Station A
Toronto, ON M5W 1P9
416-691-9519

Hotlines

Drug Abuse Information
  and Treatment Line
1-800-662-HELP
(Spanish) 800-66-AYUDA

Drug and Alcohol Hotline
1-800-252-6465

Glossary
Explaining New Words

amphetamine Drug that speeds up the
  functions of the brain and body.
bummer A bad experience, or "bad trip,"
  from using a drug.
hallucinogen Drug that upsets the
  chemicals in the brain, causing the
  user to see, hear, smell, and behave
  differently.
high The effects of a hallucinogen on the
  user.
hooked State of being addicted to a drug.
LSD Lysergic acid diethylamide, a strong
  human-made hallucinogenic drug.
MDMA Human-made hallucinogenic drug
  containing a mix of both LSD and
  amphetamines; also called *ecstasy*.
magic mushroom Mushroom (fungus)
  containing *psilocybin*, a hallucinogen.

mescaline Natural chemical that is a hallucinogen; found in the peyote cactus plant.

overdose Too much of a drug, causing sickness or death.

PCP Phencyclidine, the most dangerous human-made hallucinogen.

peyote Cactus plant whose top "button" contains mescaline, a hallucinogenic drug.

psilocybin Natural chemical that is a hallucinogenic drug found in "magic mushrooms."

THC Tetrahydrocannabinol, a common hallucinogenic chemical found in marijuana.

tripper A person who has upset the chemicals in his or her brain by using a drug.

For Further Reading

Algeo, Philippa. *Acid and Hallucinogens*. New York: Franklin Watts, 1990.

Anonymous. *Go Ask Alice*. New York: Simon & Schuster, 1971.

Ball, Jacqueline A. *Everything You Need to Know About Drug Abuse*, rev. ed. New York: Rosen Publishing Group, 1994.

Berger, Gilda. *Addiction*. New York: Franklin Watts, 1992.

Condon, Judith. *The Pressure to Take Drugs*. New York: Franklin Watts, 1990.

Johnson, Gwen and Rawls, Bea O'Donnell. *Drugs and Where to Turn*. New York: Rosen Publishing Group, 1993.

Shulman, Jeffrey. *Focus on Hallucinogens*. Frederick, MD: Twenty-First Century Books, 1991.

Index

About the Authors

Ann Ricki Hurwitz holds a BA in Linguistics from the University of Colorado. Sue Hurwitz holds an MA in the Education from the University of Missouri. They are coauthors of eighteen short stories and a social studies textbook for young adults.

Photo Credits

Cover Photo: Stuart Rabinowitz
Photos on pages 2, 17, 20, 22, 27, 32, 48, 51, 56: Dru Nadler;
page 8: Photo Researchers, Inc. © Allan D. Cruickshank;
pages 13, 37, 40: Stuart Rabinowitz; page 30: Mary Lauzon;
pages 45, 52: AP/Wide World.

Design: Blackbirch Graphics, Inc.